TO: Bil

FROM:
DeVeata
LadyVee DaPoet
Williams

Thank you! :)

I personally dedicate this book to:

My parents - Mr. And Mrs. Tony & Berenice Williams
My sister - Mrs. Voltrina Hawes
My brothers - Rashard Williams & Ryan Tyeler Williams
My grandmothers - Dorothy Mae Williams
& Mary Jones Williams

and

My true friends that always believed in me -
Krystal Terrell
Nathan Sutton
Christopher Danner
Demetrius Fluker
Michael Williams
Benjamin Nelson
Raymond Maze
Toye Watts
JMG Realty, Inc. Corporate Office employees
Rhian Swain- Giboney of Red Wolf Marketing
and the Creative Goddesses of Augusta

INTRODUCTION

You are about to embark upon a journey that you are well familiar with. This is a journey through a typical existence. A continuous learning process that will cause you to relate, ponder, laugh, reminisce, and reflect. In this collection of poetic verse I have let my imagination run free in order to describe 5 areas the world has opened my eyes to. Each area of my story, your story, our story….is put into words my soul felt and my pen spoke.

The first area, and first chapter, is dedicated to "Life" itself. These poems emphasize how I found my unique self through the bombardment of stereotypes and the constant pressure to blend in with the crowd and slowly fade away. While everyone else found comfort in being one with the "in crowd" I was constantly trying to stand apart. By doing this, I found that my "trend of the moment" was a gift God gave to me and it didn't matter what other people thought. It only mattered that I did "me" to the best of my ability.

The second chapter is about the positive side of "Love" and all the joy it can bring. Once you begin to love the unique life you've created for yourself, your heart is free to be open to someone else. This mate will hopefully love you for being yourself everyday and appreciate you for all the qualities only you can bring to their life.

When it comes to being in a serious relationship, sometimes love and "Heartache" go hand and hand. The third area I focus on is about the struggles your heart goes through while in love. These thoughts plagued my mind to the point of "verbal imagination overload" and the only relief was to pour the overflow out onto paper, accept it, and move on.

In the fourth chapter I found myself in "Art". I used poetry as a creative outlet for sharing my emotions, often with spoken word performance poetry, and I realized that others related to the issues I was going through. After going through heartache you might find yourself listening to your favorite music, drawing pictures of your dreams, or even writing hate letters no one will ever see just to clear your head of the situation. Artistic outlets have a way of cleansing our hearts of pain and opening our minds to new possibilities.

After all is said and done, we often find ourselves in a state of "Observations and Reflections". The final chapter consists of random thoughts about the world around you when you are finally free to see things with an open mind. When we let go of other people's expectations of us and start living by our God-ordained purpose, a figurative multi-colored light illuminates all the areas on our life's journey.

For the first time ever, I've looked into your eyes. Your hand is placed in mine. We've come this far on our life journey together. Now it's time to turn the page….

Table of Contents

Life– Finding Myself Amongst the Chaos

"My Strength"	2
"Being a Woman"	4
"In the Midst of All the Quiet"	5
"Geisha GrrL"	6
"Proof of Life"	7
"I'm the Best Company I've Ever Met"	8
"Same Streets"	10
"Building Up the Girl"	11
"Will They Be There?"	13
"The City is Calling"	14

Love– The Inspirations of Seduction

"Candy Shop"	16
"Unspoken Love"	17
"What Love Should Feel Like"	18
"February 14th"	19
"The Party"	20
"Natural Attraction"	21
"The Gift the Creator Gave Me"	22
"Weekend Sunrise"	23
"Heart Sponge"	24
"Us…Right Now"	25

Heartache– The Realization of Love Lost

"Love Hurts Like an Ice Cream Headache"	28
"Won't Have You"	29
"Relationship Apathy"	31
"California Insomnia"	32

"Broken All Apart"	34
"Hope you Realize"	35
"Flashbacks of You"	36
"I'm Missing You like the Rain"	37
"You Remember"	38
"Death of Love"	39

Art– The Art and Love of Poetic Expression

"Expression"	42
"I Haven't Written a Poem in a Real Long Time"	44
"How and Why the Poetry Comes"	45
"A Poet's Life"	47
"To Love a Poet"	48

Observations and Reflections
Random Thoughts that Reveal the World

"Noise"	50
"Same Page"	51
"Mary Janes"	52
"The King's Men"	53
"Evoking Inspiration"	54
"Round World, Square Life"	55
"Homeless"	56
"Reflection"	57
"Sunrise"	58
"My Skin"	59
"Dancing Queen"	60
"Graduation Day"	61
"Other Interests"	62
"Religiosity"	63
"New Day"	64
Acknowledgments	65

LIFE –
Finding Myself Amongst the Chaos

"My Strength"

That little girl in faded jeans—tight ponytail frazzled by the wind.
I'd climb in trees. Notice me.
I wanted to be your son. I'd make good grades.
Notice me. Make me the important one.
Tell me that you love me, hug me every once in a while
Or just pat me on the head. Even that would make me smile.
Look at my magic trick.
I'm invisible when you can't seem to hear me cry.
I don't know why you've left me in this room
All alone here by myself.

That young girl desperate for affectionate gestures
Or a sign to show you care.
I was there, will be here always
Your girlfriend, lover, fool.
Take my food, my car, my money
Just remember my kiss goodnight
So I can dream that I'm the important one.
Tell me that you love me, hug me every once in a while
Or just pat me on the head. Even that would make me smile.
Check out my magic trick.
I still want your love even though you make me cry.
I don't know why you've left me in this room
All alone here by myself.

That woman became a puppet with brightly colored strings–
Revlon ribbons tied with L'oreal lace
Addicted to material things.
Anything to make you happy, I'll save up to make you smile.
Give me a title to make me feel important if only for awhile.
He told me that he loved me,
Even hugged me every once in a while
Took me to grown up places and criticized me like a child.
I am pure magic now.
I've learned wisdom from past life fairy tales.
I depend on <u>me</u>. I love <u>myself</u>…
And through it all
My strength prevails.

"Being a Woman"

I can make cars slow down and eyes glance out of side windows.
I can make a man's mind wonder what's the content of my thoughts.
I can make you want to kiss my hand and not even have a reason.
I am woman—the object of your desire.

I can make 12 tasks mold in to 1 without breaking a sweat.
I can manage and supervise a group of people without them feeling inferior.
I may not change the world, but <u>my</u> world is organized, stylish and complete.
I am woman—the master of my success.

I can understand anyone through the power of my emotions.
I can quickly tell a liar from the flicker of sarcasm in the eyes.
I can see right through a fake smile or a kiss with no feeling.
I am woman—my heart is more valued than gold.

I can be royalty to the man who's chosen to be my king.
I can be everything to those who are worth my time.
I am always aware of the infinite power of my femininity.
It is up to you to take notice and give the ultimate respect.

"In the Midst of All the Quiet"

In the midst of all the quiet
You got an inner riot
Telling you to get up and break the silence.
Take a step. Try to intercept.
Try to break the mold.
Remember what the past done told.
Learn from mistakes, reiterate, back up…
Let's try again.
Looking out for true friends,
I can count them all on one hand.
I trust the chosen few that understand and comprehend
What I'm going through.
Try to find meaning
In the looking glass I'm looking through.
Can you see the inner grief that's there
Looking back at me wondering how I can pull myself
Up out of this rut?_
Take a step out of line before my time
Runs completely out.
I hear them shout across the fence
With the greener grass.
I try to sleep to let it pass but it never fails…
Dreams turn into fairytales.
Fear tells me not to go, what about an obstacle?
What about what people think? What about my future goals?
Let them sink and fade away? Wait another day?
Then the way to escape might be gone.
I'd sing a sad song.
Can't go along with what might have been.
I want my NOW to be remembered in the end.
Let me send this message out to you…
Rise up from where you are
To plan for what you <u>could</u> do.

"Geisha Grrl"

Pure silk cloth embossed with Asian floral
Flows over her curves like water.
Maroon, navy, an explosion of yellow
A kaleidoscope kimono against a dark undertone.
Hard, wooden soles adorn her feet of grace.
A pedestal for a statue of complete perfection.
Midnight black hair pours over petite, rounded shoulders—
A vision in the mirror beautiful enough to be feared.

She ventures into the twilight alone
Carrying a seductive glance
And a coy, yet strategic, smile.
Pretended romantic episodes play in her mind
Under this starry sky and bright opulent moon.
One can only hope to be her chosen one…

Her amusement will make you believe
You are the only one in the world.
The softness of her hands beg and plead,
Only for a moment, to be held.
This dainty velvet flower soaked in stinging alcohol
Intoxicates your heart
And wets your soul
With crystal tears.

"Proof of Life"

From the second I wake up, from the moment I make my first choice, from the second of my 1st decision of every minute of every hour of every section of my already tedious day <u>proving myself</u> to those around me—

Showing them I'm better than what their eyes can see. How can I prove to you that I'm not pretending? I'm really like this, all shiny and new. I think like a Goddess so I can be better than you. Read textbooks and research articles, study microscopic scientific particles, take tests and quizzes to get a high grade to prove that my studying isn't in vain.

I can't explain myself. Constantly proving myself, convincing myself that who I'm pretending to be is really who I am. Create an ideal image in my mind then lotion and shine myself up. Paint my nails, brush my hair, pick scars off my face to try so hard to be that beautiful queen that dances in my dreams smiling because she's so lucky to be perfect. Scrubbing all the dirt off, putting everything in it's place, telling people only the things I decide to let them know.

Can't show them everything, not even ½ the things because if one domino falls, the whole wall will come crashing down. Then who will be there to help me pick up the pieces?

One day I'll realize
When I'm done proving myself to you
That I'm the only one
I have to prove myself to.

"I'm the Best Company I've Ever Met"

Do yo' thang 'cause I'm go do mine!
I'm the best company I know
Can't stop this flow that keeps going on and on.
For so long I thought my happiness was bought
From you and him and her and them
But then I got caught up in a moving whirlwind
Of blessed quiet.
The aloneness was so tight
That I heard it popping in my ears.
A solitary tear closed the chapter of my past.
I realized at last that I <u>can</u> be alone.
When that phone don't ring, a recreational feeling
Takes over my time and realigns my mind.
I am thrown in a place where mine is the prettiest face
God ever created.
I'm not performing, entertaining, adjusting, or falsating
Anything for anybody 'cause I'm good enough for me.
The temperature's fine, the jokes are funny…
It's fine in wind, clouds, and when it's sunny
The music is loud to what <u>I</u> want to hear.
I can drive as far as far goes or as close as what's near
And I'm not explaining. No one's complaining.
I'm not rearranging my life for anyone!
I have just begun to LOVE the me I have become
'Cause I'm the best company I've ever met.

No regrets, no looking back,
No wishing I'd said this or that,
No apologies…no chance to freeze up
And be mad over petty arguments.
Just to chill with myself has become the ultimate.
I'm easy to please, know exactly what I like.
When things don't go right, just drop and try a new idea!
So real to me I don't need a 2nd party.
So when he or she ain't here it's a cause to be sad?!
Not when I'm the best company that I've ever had.

"Same Streets"

I'm tired of driving the same streets everyday.
The same traffic at 8 am going to the same job
Every morning being late the exact time I chose to be
Late to make me even later.
The same trees fly by my window
Blooming the flowers I don't have time
To enjoy.
We're all racing to make it to a place where
We spend most of our day to make money
That we can't stay awake long enough to spend.
No time for breakfast, work through lunch,
Stay overtime and forget what "free" is.
I think the same thoughts navigating this same life
Take the identical wrong turns everyday and hoping
For a different outcome.
Maybe it <u>is</u> the same tree on the corner
That's been there for 400 years but maybe today
The sun will sparkle through a different leaf and stem.
Maybe today the street will lead me to where
I actually want to go!
Maybe this second I could choose to completely
Turn my car around and take the scenic route
To enlighten my spirit - to awaken my mind.
Maybe one day I'll be brave enough
To finally stand up and forget what
The crowd finds acceptable.
I'll rename the streets, kick off my shoes,
And dare the willing to follow <u>me</u>.
To control my destiny
I must remember confidently
That a journey of 1,000 miles begins
With a made up mind.

"Building Up the Girl"

Swinging from monkey bars
Upside down letting the blood rush to my head.
Running. Spinning in circles on a merry-go-round
Getting drunk by the world turning around me.
Red rover come on over, race towards arms
That clothesline and knock the wind right out of your body.
Swirling, silver, blurry. Awaken a whole new you.
Smiling because you made it back.
Happy because you made it back.

Strong little girl. Crying, jumping out of windows
Playing in the mud little girl. Dancing, girl scouting
Yelling, screaming, shouting little girl to get your
Undivided attention.
Not sure what change or effect it would have
If I got it. Just wanted to see how your face would change
If you saw me smile –
To see if your face would change at all.

Falling from protectedness. Living with you yet living alone.
No more friends on the playground.
Not good enough to be loved.
Fight. Call for help. Rejected. Brought back. Kissed.
Pushed. Spat at. Hugged. Caressed. Loved. Ignored.
Tired of you. Get rid of you. Get back to me.
What about me?
Whatever <u>happened</u> to me?!

Situations and circumstances
The fancy promenades and dances of life
Draining strength.
Shrinking the boldness that used to reside
Makes one want to harbor and hide
Behind soft-spoken words…
Downcast eyes.

I have to realize my own worth and size.
I'm bigger than what you made me.
I see now my own best friend.
Have to build up again.
Build myself back up again.
Build myself back up again.

"Will They Be There?"

Will they come to see me when I lay me down to rest?
Will there be anyone to put a rose upon my chest?
Will anyone remember? Will there still be time to care?
Will anyone make sure certain people and things are there?
My hair. Will they fix it just like I used to do?
My clothes. Will they dress me and put on my favorite shoes?
Will the chapel be packed with my family and friends?
Will anyone cry when it's really my end?....
Or will they shrug me off like they did when I was living?
My heart's grown cold. Will my spirit feel like forgiving
All the hard looks, deceitful ways and cold stares?
I wonder if anyone will have to be paid to be there.
Will the day be sunny, cold, or hot?
Will my family thank the strangers that show up that I've forgot?
Will there be enough money to make it really nice?
Will I have known enough good friends to make that sacrifice?

Will I get to see him again and be amazed at how
Articulate he sounds as he reads me the scriptures and finally
Tells me what they were meant to mean?
Will God give me one last chance to apologize?
Will I be able to walk in unconditional love instead of
Chasing after temporary affection with various strings tightly attached?
Will anyone miss me enough to shed a tear?
Will they be there?

I hope so…

"The City is Calling"

That highway sign tempts me every time.
I see it shine in my headlights…
Atlanta.
Just two hours away to take a trip and stay
Where the flowers are red and the concrete
Is grey…
Atlanta.
A concert booms every weekend and it's just downtown.
Just open your window and hear the city sounds.
The Marta will drive you way far or so near.
Open your eyes so your soul can hear –
Atlanta.
Everyone talks the "southern grammar" but dresses like Hollywood.
Traffic backed up for miles but if I had the gas
I know I would
Sneak out for a day, a month, a year.
J.D. says "people don't visit they move out here" to
Atlanta.
You can get a Gucci bag for under 50 bucks
While a gypsy at Underground tells you about luck
Or ride a Six Flags coaster and pray it gets stuck
Then go to Club 112 with your shirt neatly tucked - in
Atlanta.
One day I'll get there and shine
Just like the city lights.
My smile will glow as I take in the sights.
I'll save up my cash to spend all day and all night
in Atlanta….

LOVE –
The Inspirations of Seduction

"Candy Shop"

Your skin seduces me in firelight shadows.
Caramel - smooth yet firm curves of skin
Puts me in this mood I'm in.
My fingers reach out to massage.
Each lick reveals a taste so sweet.
You are my irresistible treat.
My chocolate ice cream topped with whipped cream
Laying there anxiously waiting to receive.
I wish to tie you up quick with
Cinnamon spice licorice sticks
And cover your neck with Hershey's kisses.
Each touch melts your brown skin
With that of my own.
I stroke you long and slow
To stretch the moments of time.
My tongue will savor your body
As a candy coated dessert.
This candy shop is ours
And baby, you are mine.

"Unspoken Love"

Wrap me up in your arms and I take in the love
That is forever silent -
Never spoken but I feel it all around me
As I bury my head against your chest.
Your heart beats a rhythm of romance and desire
As you close your eyes.
Inhale and exhale the love that lives between us
And builds a warm, gentle breeze that rolls over us together.
I will never long for anything other than this.
To hear you speak and put my heart at rest-
To feel like your princess
Just call me "your highness"
And I become special when no one else is around.
This is our time, free from distraction.
The world disappears.
The TV is off.
The rain and nature lull us to sleep in sweet bliss
And I'll never long for anything
Other than this.

"What Love Should Feel Like"

I have no desire for politically correct romance.
The romance that is taught on reality shows-
Awkward silences, predetermined pick up phrases,
First date representatives, buying me dinner out of obligation,
Making me laugh through conversations
Because my smile just turns you on…

I want a love that sparks my inner imagination-
Someone that knows and hungers for every side of me
Unconditionally.
No judgement, just appreciation for multifaceted differences
And how much we can learn together.
Forever intertangled in a love that won't let go.
A slow glance and the understandment is met
And we wish and long for nothing else in the world.
I need a love that can touch <u>and</u> feel-
A real lay in a tub of rose petals love and let our eyes
Close and our minds and hearts open wide kind of love.
A love that's not afraid to be spoken
Whispering softly over and over in my ear
So when our lives pull us apart
My heart will always recollect.
Oh, to moan deep from the soul and
Each time feeling like the first time kind of love.
If it's meant to be, I'm ready
But if not…
I still can dream.

"February 14th"

Overpriced, chocolate candy hearts can be sold
For more money than what they're worth to anyone
Wanting to prove that you can buy affection
From a local corner store.
Create a circus, helium, flamboyant mirage with
Red, pink, and white balloons blown up bigger than
What they need to be screaming "I LOVE YOU!!!"
Floating lifelessly in the air waiting to be shrunken and deflated
When the string gets too tired of flying.
Or better yet, try to make me into a little girl and
Surprise me with a big, fat, furry, monkey, gorilla, tiger or teddy bear
Holding a gigantic, fuzzy heart that's probably
Way bigger than I think yours will ever be
So I can not have anywhere to put it in my room
And feel guilty when I give it to charity at the end of the year.
No.
Don't tie me up in the silliness of "store bought" love.
I value your kindness and attention more than
Any tangible surprise.
Looking deep in your eyes I can see things no gift
Can ever tell me
And priceless moments like those
Can be had on any day of the year.

"The Party"

There's a beat that travels through the air
Whips my hair around and puts sparkles in my eyes
And the strides of my steps as I walk across the floor with you.
Hand in your hand I just can't stand still
Because you move me internally and outwardly
Your touch graces my hips and my lips part in ecstacy.
This is, will be, our song for the moment.
I know later all I'll remember is this
Swirling, turning, feeling-
This unbelieving that I could be a princess
In an instant in your arms.
I'm not ready yet you steady my heart as we sway
In the middle of the oasis of sound.
All around eyes are watching, wishing, hoping
To get into a groove like we've found.
A natural star kissed night with the big
Bright moon shining down.
A stroke of fate brought us here alone
And now together sharing stories and getting
To know the lives we feel compelled to bring closer.
We have each other in this dance
And like a butterfly escapes from a child's glass jar
For it's own freedom to claim -
I'm left here on this dance floor
And I was not blessed with your name.

"Natural Attraction"

One voice, one people
One love, one song.
The movement moves on
And I can't believe I'm here in it.
Still fighting, still learning
Never stopping, just believing
That one day I'm gonna matter
One day…as much as you.
I want to feel that way-
Want to touch the touch you have-
For a second just leave myself
And be totally free with us.
The lust we share could mean the whole
World if you'd just let it evolve
And dissolve into your heart.
We could be like nature you and I
Each element turning and depending on
Nothing but the wind -
The winds of change to move everything back
In place.
Touch my tear stained face and let it
Roll between your fingers.
Let my water run down like an ancient waterfall.
I feel the ripple of your skin
As the tide moves in and you are mine
Not to have
But just to hold…
And that's enough.

"The Gift the Creator Gave Me"

I love the way I can be
Completely and totally with you naturally.
I, your caramel Queen, and you my
Long awaited for dream come true.
You let me see things about me that
Were always there but ignored by others
Like how the flow of my hair looks
Sexier under bed covers.
I close my eyes and imagine the passion
That stirs up inside when you talk low,
Deep and slow on the phone.
I pretend I'm holding you and you're
Caressing my inner ear with the words
Of what's to come.
I don't know why I act so shy when you
Advance towards me
To get a chance to feel and explore me.
I guess I'm scared that the flicker of your tongue
Will have me shake out of control.
You have a way of brainwashing my thoughts
So that everything I see is your face
And I could stare off into space for hours….

I wonder if your woman feels the same way I do.
If only she knew, picked up on the clues, that
When you leave your place you come over to mine
To moan and sweat and move and grind.
Licking each drop of wine from your lips-
Using my fingertips to trace the grooves in your
Hair in between your braids.
Just sit still and feel me
As we pretend how it would be
If you <u>had</u> of met me
First.

"Weekend Sunrise"

I try not to make a sound as I watch you sleeping.
You keep all your silent dreams locked up safe
Behind closed eyes.
The room's atmosphere lingers sweet with
Cinnamon wax and candy kisses.
A new day I realize and you and I are still in love.

Can't comprehend how a heart can feel so strongly
When the future's so uncertain.
How a man can give unselfishly not getting exactly
Equally in return.
After liquid, lust, and moonlight you lay so close here right beside me.
We've been through so much…
And yet we're still in love.

I wish I could understand my true feelings.
Sometimes I wish I could stop time.
My heart flows emotions like a river
Held back by the floodgates of my mind.

I know we'll always be together
If not in sight - one call away.
Our friendship is like your warm embrace -
I want to always feel this way.

"Heart Sponge"

Take a deep look at who you are inside.
Come alive and realize the wonderful
That resides underneath closed eyes.
Your spirit hungers to live the life it
Was created for. No more locked doors.
No more afraid.
No more flesh keeping you scared,
Holding you back from what's
Always been there-
Waiting just beyond your reach,
Calling to you to take that next step.
Unlock the heart that's screaming to be free.
Be with me and see the levels we can
Span together holding each other's hands
Understanding all and nothing at the same instance.
Forgetting what the world preaches and
Writing our own chapter.
Each going after a feeling we both can't define.
All I know is you are mine
And if I am yours…
Our love is complete.

"Us...Right Now"

Come into my eyes.
Look at me the way you do.
Smile as you hungrily touch me and make me
Into your woman.
I'm here, you're here
And together we define love.
We grope for each other in the dark.
We taste each other's lips and remember
How good it feels to be so close,
To forget every other thing.
Don't pleasure me. Don't perform for me -
Instead
Indulge <u>yourself</u>.
Do to me what makes <u>you</u> smile,
And moan….and sweat, and beg for it never to end.
Lock me deep into your heart, my love,
And take me
Wherever you go.

Heartache–
The Realization of Love Lost

"Love Hurts Like an Ice Cream Headache"

I had love once.
I dug gentle but deep into it
And it curled up on my silver spoon.
A cold mist rose from it like a dry ice haze-
A magical, milky coldness with a sweet sugar scent-
Light, caramel love with hundreds of hiding chocolate hearts.
The anticipation was overwhelming.
Love kissed my awaiting lips and my tongue ushered it inside.
I felt a chill down my spine that created a warmth in my stomach.
I <u>had</u> to have more.
Each spoonful scrawled a lazy grin on my face
And made my cheeks flush a bashful crimson glow.
I indulged in love over and over letting orgasmic waves
Of decadent plEaSure COMpletELy TAKE CONTROL UNTIL…
Oh!! Oh my. The pain! Make it stop! Oooo!!
How can such a delicious dessert of love
Leave a stinging…pulsating….THROBBING…that almost
Cripples me?!
Should not have fell so deep in—
My head, my heart…
The roof of my mouth is so cold.
A tension squeezes a tear that drops into an empty container.
An ache resides within me
And my love has melted away.

"Won't Have You"

It wouldn't be good for me
If you were mine.
I couldn't bear to face myself in the mirror
If you were cramping my style,
Changing my plans,
Changing my life.
Please don't kiss me
With your stained teeth that might rub off
On my perfect smile.
I can't breath your air lest it taint my own.
Don't stand near me or your sweat
Will stain my clothes.
Don't dance near me– others might think
<u>I</u> was the one bringing you joy.
People might think I was the one
Making you happy
And I want to appear available
To everyone else <u>but</u> you.
I'll wash and clean your car
Because I'm the one that's driving it.
I want everyone on the street to think
This clean ride is mine- for the moment anyway.
Let me buy you these clothes
So I won't be embarrassed when I'm with you.
Don't want people to think I hang out
With a person that dresses in a way I don't approve.

Let's fix you up – strip your identity and make
You into someone meant to keep me happy
For the short time I'm around.
Want a title? Here, take it!
Now I'll make it impossible to keep.
Make this your punishment for ever thinking
You'd have me as your very own.
All to yourself when I'm so desired?
Who in the world do you think you are?!
I'll use and abuse while you try so hard
To make me the star.
I'll use your dreams to my advantage-
Your wisdom to help _me_ prosper.
Your love for selfish pleasure.
And in the end beneath a puddle of tears
You'll put all the blame on yourself.
We'll eat when _I'm_ hungry, I'll entertain you when _I'm_ bored.
You'll think I'm giving you the world…
When all you wanted
Was my heart.

"Relationship Apathy"

Get around to me...
Why do I have to fight for the
Attention that is rightfully
Mine.
There was once a time
When I was put 1st but I'm
Now put on the back burner shine.
Last.
So quick, fast
Your to do list and tasks
Build up high in contrast
To everything that's
Us.
Try to discuss.
Don't want to put up a fuss
But sometimes I miss the frantic lust
We shared.
Friend/lover/girlfriend/
Woman/needs/friend
Silence.
No one here but
Me...
And I can be alone
All by myself.

"California Insomnia"

Blank stare
Down turned smile
A silent soundtrack trying to create the exact sound
Soft skin
Heartache
My tears sting my cheeks
As they well up in my eyes
Leaves rustle in the wind
You call me to bed
Warm
I feel the closeness of your embrace as we
Hold on in this time
Knowing it will be over soon
Darkness
Your voice like music
The night comforts us both
Makes me wish things were–
I were–
Different

Situations rearranged so I could
Stay in this time so familiar
But, my God, there's so much change
Want to plug my ears and ignore it
And hope it will go away
And I can be what my heart wants
A faint whisper of "always"
I'm smiling and I'm hurting
All this pain locked up inside
Like two hands with fingers interlocked
And one is pulling to let go
Have to be stronger than this
I know that we'll meet again soon
Trust, you'll see
Until then
Don't let your heart stop beating
Wish I could stop remembering
This oh so wonderful feeling
That can't last…

"Broken All Apart"

Your search ended with me but the game was not over.
I don't meet your standards and I probably never will.
Can't be your ideal right now. Your "everything" woman
Is still out there.
I became a sexy, still-learning obstacle.
What a debacle for you to try to make it work.
It's too good to leave behind. Too young and tender to ignore.
My potential is so perfect.
As perfect as you think <u>you</u> are.
You jumped in anyway. Screwed with my heart—
Made my mind believe.
Now the clouds are rolling away.
The truth is shining through like a glorious beam of light.
We were never supposed to dance.
It was all a mistake.
Bad timing, bad lighting…everything not in place.
Drunk. Shaking our hips to loud, blaring music
That intoxicated our judgement.
I fell and you caught me
Over and over.
Brushed me off, tried to fix me up—
No one will notice…how unhappy I really am.
Just smile.
Put your costume on and pretend.
See? They love you…
Just like I'm supposed to.
Just like you thought I would.
I had you fooled too.
It'll all work out one day.
I'll go my way and leave you here
To wonder what could have been.
Good thing I refused to be nothing more than friends.
It's so much easier to break a heart
Already in pieces.

"Hope you Realize"

When all the girls start to blend
To look and act exactly the same,
When a cold stare pierces the moment
When accidently she's called <u>my</u> name,
When no one is at fault
And there's nothing left to blame,
I hope you realize.

When there's no more tears to fall
From the corners of our eyes
And weekends spent <u>anywhere</u> but with me
Come more often with no surprise
The restless nights bring forth a memory
Of how togetherness took compromise
But that was a small price to pay
To gain so much.

A small touch, a quick hug,
A short conversation passing by..
Will that be enough to help you realize,
Fess up and finally admit
That between the both of us
There's love?

"Flashbacks of You"

I dreamt of you last night again-
That grin of yours as you walked away.
That playful, teasing, uncaring way
You messed around with my mind and fooled me to believe.
I felt your touch in my sleep last night.
Smelled your skin amidst dim bedroom light.
Reached out to you and the feeling was right-
As usual…you weren't there.
I see glimpses of you in other men on TV
And wonder if you'd be different if you were here with me.
Now after all we've learned being apart
Would you put forth the effort to make a new start
Or just be comfortable with where we left off?
A confusing series of kisses and groping in the dark
Always running and searching for what we can't define.
Trying to put together identity-
The "me" I thought was mine
Knowing all the while our lust wasn't strong enough
To make anything last.
I'll let the morning sunrise dispel and eradicate my past.
Thank God…
I'm finally waking up.

"I'm Missing You like the Rain"

I'm missing you like the rain,
The pure wetness of it all.
It glistens on my window pane
Like tears
Falling and crawling down a cheek
That used to be taut with smiling happiness.
Straining pretended gladness
Won't heal the weakness in my heart.
My nerves patter like raindrops
With just a thought of your warm touch.
Miss you so much I can see a cloud forming.
This storm that builds up with emotion
Over feeling, over longing for a moment-
Just one moment in the sun.
The winds of change have begun to blow
And I remember how you see me.
I remember how you feel me even though
I'm miles away.
I remember that one day we can recreate
And make up for all lost time.
The most comfort is derived from the simple truth
That I can use these drops of rain
To grow a flower
Just for you.

"You Remember"

The moans you so lovingly extracted
From my lungs are still ringing in your ears.
You remember me.
Invisibly I touch you like a ghost in the night
Caressing your mind, I float softly through your thoughts..
You remember.
How each kiss sent a spark of hope down
Your spine straight to your heart.
You still feel me—the intensity of our chemistry
Won't let your soul forget you and me.
So passionately we loved until two became one,
Now the dreams have begun and you can't
Help but reach out to me in your restless sleep.
Toss and turn in the bed we once shared.
Me holding on tight and stroking your hair.
You know you remember this room and that chair.
How we both cried together and hugged right there.
How we both realized that life without love wasn't fair.
So we made up and explored one another—
Through and over and under each other.
Yes, you remember.
So, why can't I forget?!

"Death of Love"

You can tell when love has left the room.
It's like closing the casket at the wake too soon.
You want one more look but their eyes are closed.
Their heart's turned off and you just know.
You feel their face and it's freezing cold.
Their body is stiff, the love's grown old.
A shell lying there void of any life or spirit.
You can yell and scream "I LOVE YOU!!!"
But no way they're gonna hear it.
They're dressed in their best clothes
But not for you.
All of a sudden they've got better "other" things to do.
Some lie there with a smile
Like they're dreaming they're not there.
Some fill their face with make up
And get a new twist to their hair.
It's like a trumpet blows in the distance
And they know it's just their time
To leave with no explanation, no last phone call
And no sign.
It's time again to be strong–
Protect my dignity at any cost.
I don't care how the saying goes.
I know it's better to be loved
Than to have lost.

Art–
The Art and Love of Poetic Expression

"Expression"

A rainbow of color is washing over me. I am feeling the brilliance
Of multi-colored streams and oceans of light.
My hands are trembling, overwhelmed with unrestrained emotion.
I just can't sit still! I want to move but I'm frozen,
Want to yell but my voice is taken,
Want to stand up and be shaken, just SCREAM to let ya'll hear me!
Do you? Can you? Will you
Listen?
I can be strong when I have to, yeah. I can make the colors
Change from *deep ocean blue* to FIRE ENGINE RED
And nod and shake my head like all the attitude bubbling up
Inside my brain is what I'm all about….but will ya'll hear me?
If I yell just to be yellin' or sing just because everyone else is singing
And throw paper on the ground and speak foul language
Got damn! Won't I lose the uniqueness that is inherently me?
Won't I be put into the mold of everything tired and old
And locked away into your forgotten experiences?
Can't fear the senses that are heightened when you
Realize the difference between just going through the motions
And giving birth to a poetic spoken word creation.
Giving each syllable an interval of feeling to make it run off the page
Into the mind that dares to entertain it.

Let me frame this runaway train. Let me contain this stream of consciousness
It's obvious that I understand
But can I stand up here and make YOU understand is the question
And the goal.
Can you see the fractured soul that these words BURST out from
To get a glimpse of sparkling daylight?
The sight of me being anything but free to say these words creatively
Would be a shame and a disgrace to the art.
It should be a rule in spoken word school to start to
Tear apart each poem after it's said
Which would force a satisfied head to come up with
A brand new idea. Move away from the comfortable.
Say something you're not sure you'll get a response to.
What's worse? To deal with the silence of a close minded audience
Or let your expression become the answer to each and every question?
You can stretch and bend your thoughts to get hand claps, daps, and praises.
Hell, throw in some plagiarized hip hop phrases
And yell and cry to put on a show.
But even if the words you wrote
Were the exact words you should have spoke
The message from what you're saying
Won't be heard.

"I Haven't Written a Poem in a Real Long Time"

The room is midnight.
Starry sky sparkles though my ½ draped window frame.
The chill crawls up the back of my legs
And prickles the hair on my arm to remind me
Of how long it's been.
I don't recall what "warm" is.
The sheets lie askew at the foot of my bed.
My eyes are fixated on the shadows that dance
On the ceiling above me.
I sprawl across the mattress to take up the space.
I'm all alone—you've left me here—
And the darkness engulfs my soul.
Crickets and streetcars play the soundtrack of the night
And remind me that life goes on whether or not
I'm part of it.
My mind is blank yet I cannot sleep.
All the words have been said, promises made and broken.
Incomplete apologies in beautifully scripted phrases
Are scrawled on almost-enveloped letters
Like confetti across the floor.
I secretly wish the party you're having without me
Is filled with haunting, regretful thoughts.
The awkward silences pushed you away.
I touch myself, the way you used to, and long for
Nothing in the world but
To be filled with an emotional outburst of creative
Lustful episodes that would spill over into
A perfectly crafted
Poem.

"How and Why the Poetry Comes"

I don't want to be the "angry black female".
Can't write a "jail poem" 'cause I've never been there.
My hair never been dreaded up enough
To script a rhyme about times growin' up on the dirty streets.
My feet are too soft to know the hard road you been travelin'.
Each line I write is unravelin' another story.
What gory details of my soap opera, fairytale life can I
Metaphorically let you explore?
Open up this door for you to see.
This poetry is what sets me free from the madness,
The sadness, the "he said–she said" craziness of it all.
Can't bring myself to delve into anything but what's real.
The poems I erect aren't politically correct.
Can't limit my words to phrases typically heard in polite
Cliches and birthday Hallmark cards.
All the hardness I know is the affairs of my heart.
When I start to be fake, my pen wobbles and shakes
Scribbles of refusal.

It's not used to pretending. It wants to be sending
The truth of what's really going on.
How long can I offend you with my words of harsh reality?
It had to be spoken if that was what I was feeling at the time.
I'd rather speak my mind about what happened then harbor
It in my soul. Can't let go of the ongoing cinema of my dreams.
My poetic mind knows no other release.
I speak of happy-go-lucky relationships but also
Those nights between the sheets can't be forgotten.
They have to be captured by the bobbing of my pen.
In the end you'll realize and thank me for finding a way to bend
The moments, the thoughts, the talks, the silent oh-my-God stares,
And glares into creative works of art.
Don't start to tell me that everything I write should be this way
Or that way or happy…
My poems are never sappy misinterpretations or re-creations of
False occurrences wrapped up in pretty paper to protect the innocent.
Be content and know that each word I write has a deserved
And earned purpose.
A lyrical wave of descriptive feeling has risen
from a blank canvas floor to an enlightened surface.

"A Poet's Life"

I got so many poems locked up in my head.
I got so many poems locked up in my head.
Can't live my life fast enough for them to be said.
Got so many poems locked up in my head.

Got rhyme after rhyme dancing in my brain.
Sometimes it's impossible for me to explain.
Forever entertaining this paper with my pain.
My life is in hiding but I'm too rich mentally to complain.
The world keeps spinning and I'm stuck in the rain
With my pen and my pad getting verbally stained.
No one seems to get this drift they think I'm going insane.
Got rhyme after rhyme dancing in my brain.

I got thought after thought brewing in my soul.
Got thought after thought brewing in my soul.
Hope I live long enough for my own story to be told.
Before my words get tired and old
I hope I can touch someone with these words in my soul.
I'd travel anywhere in the hot or even in the cold
Just to open your eyes with these words in my soul.

"To Love a Poet"

Smoky, dimly lit nightclub—
Someone plucks a bass string instrument and the music
Is interwoven throughout the room.
Tiny candles dance warm, fiery shadows
And cast a glow on each face.
Ice cubes clank against cheap wine glasses.
Microphone is quiet.
Pages from your notebook flutter and you
Confidently swagger to approach the stage.
Your eyes lock with mine.
An accident perhaps but what a spark it creates
As if it were intentional.
Talk of the love you would make
If you were lucky enough to be united with
Someone who understands the longing of a poet's soul.
My mind melts with your voice and your lips
Speak words that run fingers through my hair,
Down my back, and holds my waist in the lounge chair
I'm trying so cool to sit in
Not able to move for fear that this feeling won't last.
Breathe softly the phrases that find me through the
Club's cigarette hazes and caress my ears like a
Seductive tongue with a secret that can't wait to be told.
Take me with you in your mind as you walk off the stage.
Dream of me and this night
So that the next poem you write
Will lovingly describe
Us.

Observations and Reflections

*Random Thoughts
that Reveal the World*

"Noise"

frequency transmitting digital bits and pieces of fragmented particles of mini bites of sound in waves over and over to cloud the brain with melodic and chaotic tangles of information that your nerve cells struggle to cover their ears / to no avail the stereo feeds into the audio speaker DVDs and woofers tweeters footsteps sneakers pounding pavement wishing for a ride with a boomin' system that stems from a street connection / takes me back to when brothas held their boom box high on their shoulder and set it down on the corner for little girls to have a soundtrack to play hopscotch to / three, four, five, six chalk marks and pick up sticks these kids are yelling, singing, swimming, my head is throbbing / too much noise / I need the quiet sublime peace silence / take me to a private ocean / where the water can wash / my crowded imagination clean….

"Same Page"

It's gonna be beautiful— the day, the time, the place
When we can put down barriers and look each other in the face
And see way past the differences and see we're all the same.
We all been there all playin' the same game.
Each a bundle of emotions all tied up tight.
Everything is fine then nothing's just quite right.
All reaching for the future. Some running from the past.
Some squinting like a China man through a looking glass.
Some got goals and the foot action to make 'em happen.
Just slap a plan up and then stand up and watch the audience
Get to clappin'. My hand's up in the front row
Trying to get the teacher's attention.
It's my turn now. How loud do I have to mention
For you to finally hear me?!
My resume's right here!
Type the cover letter and hope and pray
You don't cover your ears.
I walk with no fear 'cause my God walks before me
And gives the open door to my awaiting destiny see
I'm focused, centered, if you can feel me then fine
If not, it's all good, just don't cut ahead of me in line.
Got my eyes set straight. I just can't wait…
Til the world wipes the crust off
And wakes up on the same page.

"Mary Janes"

It glistens in the moonlight-
The patent leather gleams under the sparkle of the stars.
The soft strap across the arch of my foot suggests
A girl I never knew named "Mary Jane"…
Wide chunky heels.
Who was this woman? Why are my shoes named after her?
She must have been short, this girl, to need such chunky heels
To tower over everyone.
She must have been shy to have to use her shoes for
A new self-confident existence.
She must have been…just like me.

Sitting on this park bench after the concert
I swing the shoes in the wind.
Streaks of black onyx blurring the grey concrete beneath me.
She was mysterious…this Mary Jane.
She wore glimmering diamond chokers and feather boas
With her indigo jeans just to
Make people wonder.

She wore shiny, patent leather shoes of every style
To every function of her life and it
Inspired someone so much as to name the shoe after her.
I own and wear her shoes and embody her spirit.
Staring up in the sky I can see my herbal smoke
Take her figure as she slowly walks away.

"The King's Men"

All of us,
Every last one of us
Maneuvering our heavy, tin can armor
Must come to this gigantic, stupid wall
Every day
Carrying our glue, and tape, and thread
Sent to this wall by the king
Riding our bucking horses over
Woodland and plain
Just to rescue
The alcoholic Humpty Dumpty
Who falls off the same wall
In a drunken eggnog stupor
With a fractured grin
Zigzagged around his face.

"Evoking Inspiration"

A small, light ball sun of color
sits on the table
like thoughts in my head.

Slippery, juice packets festering feeling
are tightly enclosed inside
a rubbery shell of skin-
still ripe green on one side.

Imagination juices swim freely
all closed up in this tiny sphere of time.
My paper waits for inspiration.

I raise my pen to break the juices free.
JAB, STAB, and PICK! Tension…POWER…release.
The leathery shell bursts with each poke.

The thoughts drain down and drench my paper.
The juices trickle down creatively
and make the sticky puddle of
a poem.

"Round World, Square Life"

I am the puzzle piece that tries so hard to fit in.
My mind, it transcends to take me up higher
But each day I try to pull myself back down.
Want to be on your level speaking southern slang,
A bit disheveled 'cause that ghetto thang is "in" now.
Errybody wanna be dat down azz chic.
Can't fit or squeeze my various personalities into a mold
You conveniently crafted and created for me.
You'd adore me and be all chummy if my life was
Slow like yours.
Being hit with obstacles and closed doors to the point
You just give up.
I can't corrupt my life that way just to have
30 pages on my phone each day talking
Cool and close to nothing just to say I'm not alone.
I'd rather put my phone on silent
To try to find where my woman inside went
We can chill and talk real frequent
'Cause she's the <u>only</u> friend I trust.

"Homeless"

I'm out of breath from running.
Sweat pours down my skin and mixes with my tears.
People walk by holding hands and smiling.
The wind that breezes by me sends a shiver down my spine.
I'm shaking in the dark in this lonely, gloomy alley
And I hate the very fact that I've been here
Many times before.
Left alone with my head down fixated on unclean shoes
With my hair frazzled to resemble the turmoil in my head.
I carry my baggage with me.
Every bad experience of my past that people use to define me
Is tied up in plastic bags. I carry them with me
Wherever I go.
No one sees me anymore. They see my situation.
They analyze the bad choices of my past and assume
I'm not capable of change.
I'm curled up in the shadows so no one can see me tremble.
I've been chasing love all day.
In this race to the finish line of your affection
I can't seem to move out of the very last place.

"Reflection"

Paint away the shadows
The crows around the eyes
Try to look warm and natural underneath
Let the heat bend and mold your hair into submission
Lay it down slow
Heart beats fast
Lips are red, just like the nails
Bright, white smile
Pressed clothes
Pretty, pretty sunshine
Cameras flash
Have a look for each emotion
Exaggerate, then hold back
Take it in, then push it away
A different smile for everyday
Camera one then camera two
Stare at your perfection, your reflection
Your image you've…they've..created
Complete and whole, every sequin
Sparkles golden, glittering light enough to
Blind your thoughts
Complete on the outside
But inside—
A shattered glass.

"SUNRISE"

It's 7 am.
The world rolls back the dark cover of night and everyone begins again.
Another chance to get it right. Choices, decisions…
Will I sleep through the alarm or sit straight up and look the day
Right in the eyes?
It's all on me. If not today…when?
My spirit forces my flesh to slowly move.
The show begins and old ladies sweep the dust off their doorsteps.
The gossip from last night can be heard from way down the road.
My childhood stirs in my mind.
I see the school kids sit on electrical boxes to wait for their bus
Half asleep with backpack, lunch box, and carefully combed hair.
A tall brunette with a smirk on her face leads a pack of white
Methodist children across the street.
They are all dressed the same—white shirt, navy slacks, plaid skirt.
Everyone wears brown shoes. No black faces,
Scrubbed crisp and clean.
No one is smiling.

Riding down the street behind industrial vans driving slow on
The company's time clock.
Restaurants filling the air with warm smells of grilled meat
And fried chicken.
I will embrace this day like a forgotten lover
That has decided to change
And make the most of our time together.

"My Skin"

I love the skin I'm in.
Light skinned, caramel, the red boned,
Pecan-tan of it all. I love the toasty, Caribbean,
Sun-kissed glow my skin has in the summer
And the brown, porcelain doll I become in the fall.
My ageless black beauty will never get old
Because that's the way God made me.
He chose me to be the color of ocean-kissed sand.
These auburn lines of time that run through my hands
Are "character marks" and they spark stories
Of the struggles and the pain.
Years of "making ends meet" again and again.
I pulled, yanked, and forced those ends into a tightly bound bow.
My skin is my strength, I let everyone know.
Even those that try to shun me 'cause my flesh is lighter than the norm.
I don't succumb to ignorance and to them I don't conform.
Feel free to shut me out and doubt my "blackness"
'cause I'm not as dark as you. I'll shine alone regardless
Being the very <u>best</u> me in spite of you.

"Dancing Queen"

Look at me.
Look hard enough to stare.
See my body move but you will never see my eyes.
I dance to the rhythm we've both created together.
You'll never approach me even after long contemplation
And overcoming of fear.
I am the disco jewel that shines and sparkles in all
My mystery.
You wonder if by fate I came here alone.
Sipping free drinks and water to coincide
With the beads of sweat that have gathered on my skin.
A cool breeze blows in and you wish to share my space.
From across the room you rock and step as if pretending
A dance with me from long distance range.
Isn't it strange that we are so like-minded but you remain
So far away?
No matter though as the night goes on—
You depart with longing
Yet I'm fully satisfied.

"Graduation Day"

This journey. This chapter. This road of life I'm traveling…
Full of risk, uncertainty, full of hope.
I know I'm in oh so deep in my sleep. I dream
Of where I can't seem to get right now.
Don't know how but trusting God will tell me
In his own time.
Not mine, His time…can't wait sometime
But I know it's better to sit and let
Chips fall where they may and then I'll place
The pieces together.
The puzzle comes with no directions.
No help.
Nobody to turn to but me.
Put rose-colored glasses on my contacted glazed eyes
To see a better future than what I'm living currently.
It's kinda hazy. Folks think I'm crazy just thinking out loud.
Being proud of accomplishments as farther and further
I went outside the obstacle box of conformity.
The door, you see, has been slowly yet wondrously
Opened for me.
Now all I have is my own 2 feet
To confidently walk on through.

"Other Interests"

We could always begin anew.
Brand new day, small talk and number
Trying to pretend that his jokes are as funny
And her smile is as warm as mine.
Sip wine over candlelight and try to find comfort
In a stranger's eyes
Who might just be who you want them to be.
For the moment, everything's all good.
It's understood that every Friday night
We could dress like we were going out
Together in separate clubs across the country
Hoping the next person that walks to the dance floor
Will be you
Or someone like you with the way we are.
Maybe I could tell him what to say, how to hold me just that way
And I'll replace his face with yours.
Or maybe she'll be just like me but
A little bit more certain
Just a tad bit more perfect
But how boring <u>that</u> would be.

I lie in bed alone remembering
Our wonderful past fantasies.
I know our soon to be reality
Is more than enough to wait for.

"Religiosity"

Glory to God! Glory in the highest!
Please Lord let me have the flyest suit on next Sunday so the front pew folks can say "Man, look how fine and holy **that** one is!"
Let me borrow hers or his Bible so I can prove my spiritual point anointing the scriptures with my interpretation
Don't interrupt my mind elevation while I flip each verse and scripture to make it mean what I need to say.
We pray and worship the same Lord but my church clique cooler than ya'lls.
The walls of our minds are smaller. One mere compromise equates a fall.
We gonna ball 'cause God made us wealthy. We'll ignore that He also said to give
not only money but an open heart so those that seek shall also live.
But instead we'll boast <u>our</u> talents and a holy spotlight will warm <u>our</u> feet.
God shakes His head looking down from heaven…
Glory to God…
or glory to me?

"New Day"

I disappeared from a few.
Gotta do that sometime.
Took a pilgrimage to a different place
A new time.
Erased a few people from my past
To get a new start.
Asked the "Most High" to cleanse
My mind and my heart.
Forgave a few folks.
Some I forgave without them knowing.
I had trust in too many…
Behind their smiles, their horns were showing.
From the confusion and the stress
I chose to walk away.
I take the simple route now. My inner child comes out to play.
I censor what I speak as not to overwhelm.
I dare not get too deep– I'll unconsciously lose myself
In a whirlwind of thoughts, ideas and phrases…
Have me hunting my pen down to script a few pages.
Yes, I opened up my mind so my soul could hear.
The morning sun is finally shining
And my future's bright and clear.

Acknowledgments

I would like to thank the following people that inspired me and supported me throughout my journey to creating this poetry collection. God, first and foremost, in my mind is not a "person" so I praise and thank Him constantly above all else for blessing me with the gift of creative, poetic verse. Others I would like to acknowledge are:

My family: I rebelled against my parent's authority. They yelled at me and forgave me anyway. My mother taught me to be calm to get through my mistakes and that a smile will open doors when a smart mouth might get you slapped. My father and sister taught me to be cool and strong in every situation and to find the humor in life. My brother, God rest his soul, taught me to be honest about your abilities and always try to surpass what people think you can do. Lastly, my grandmothers taught me style, resourcefulness, spirituality, and tact. The poems in this collection could not have been written without the inspiration and lessons taught to me by my family.

My friends:

Krystal– Always the best friend that didn't give up on friendship after high school. Love you, chica! You found true love and I would only hope to do the same one day. IWA for Life!

Nathan- You said I could do anything I set my mind to. You also said you wished the best for me. Thank you for showing me worlds I would have never known and emotions deep enough to create wonderful poetry.

Chris- Even though you stole my journal that day and ran around my apartment complex while I ran after you trying to get it back, I still appreciate you being not only a fan of my poetry, but a fan of my life in general. Your encouragement and love is well noted in my journal and on my heart as well.

Demetrius- Thank you. Thank you a million times over…for everything. You are amazing and every moment with you is too short. Your smile, kindness, and love lights up my life and my poetry book is complete because of you.

Mike- If I ever needed a friend, your ear was open to hear my request. Thank you for taking a chance with me and helping me see how much potential I had to be so much more than what I was.

Ben- The nights of "body/brain washing" and the creepy way we found each other again after so much time, and then vanished from each other again is beyond my current understanding. From so far away, you supported my poetry, and my most secret thoughts, and I appreciate that. Forever I'll be, your Annabel Lee.

Ray- You taught me to take the situations in my life and turn them exactly how I know they should go. You believed in me back in the day and you inspired me to put "feet to my dreams". With the right hustle, anything is possible…

Toye- Looking over all the poems you wrote me in the past, I truly believe our hearts were in the same place for a season. I could always count on you to clap the loudest after my spoken word and that encouragement means the world to me.

JMG- You guys are great! Being independent in Atlanta isn't so bad when you have a work family of friends that support you and your craft. Thank you!

Rhian- The "Ice Cream Poem" is in the book!! The Creative Goddesses of Augusta have really made me feel special from day one. I raise my golden wand and tilt my diamond tiara to the love of artistic expression!

And last but not least, I'd like to thank Terry Spratt and the creative crew of Authorhouse.com for believing in me and helping me publish this first collection of poetry.

A new day I realize
And me and poetry
Are still in love…

Made in the USA
Lexington, KY
11 April 2010